Women
Working
Wonders
Wednesdays

RainBlue

DEDICATION

This is to all the women living today and in the future.
Thank-you for caring enough to make the world a better place to live now and long after we're each gone!

CONTENTS

ACKNOWLEDGMENTS

Who do you acknowledge in this? It seems to be the same acknowledgment each time. I thank God and the Universe for helping me make the world a better place to live! Thank-you to family and friends who graciously put up with my endless ideas and chatter too!

1 INTRODUCTION

For probably decades, but definitely the last eight years, main stream media has been opinionating and not reporting. The opinionating is also very Democrat leaning. This leaning allows the media to help divide "We the People". In my experience, mainstream media more often than not loves Democrats and demonizes everyone else.

Instead of always presenting the Democrat's approval or disapproval side depending on the Democrat's position of an issue, the mainstream media should be reporting pros, cons, and all positions. Report what the Democrat's position is both pro and con. Then report what the Republican's position is both pro and con. If there are other positions, present them both pro and con. Do this at the same time. That is in the same report or program. At the end of the presentation, the only question would then be, "What do you think?" Allowing "We the People" to make-up our own informed, educated minds. As it is currently in 2017, "We the People" need to read and watch multiple sources. Many of us just don't have the time! We're busy attending college, working, raising our children, and hoping to enjoy doing these for a happy life. The mainstream media knows this too and won't likely change any time soon.

It has been my experience that MSNBC is extremely left, Democrat opinion. CNN was very pro Hillary Clinton which is why they garnered the nickname: Clinton News Network. For those who don't know, they were caught giving Hillary debate questions during the 2016 election cycle. CNN might claim they didn't know about the employee who did this at the time, but ultimately she was their employee. Said employee was fired only after "We the People" found out and made known our disapproval! Since the 2016 election and exposure of "Fake News", CNN does seem to be moderating back toward the center. However, I don't trust them! They are still overall Democrat leaning. Some of their reporters more than others lean Democrat. It's getting easier for me to see the differences as of April 2017.

To be fair and practice what I preach, Fox News leans Republican. Sometimes they should be more upset about what Republicans or the right are doing! What I've seen is a calmer reporting of what the Democrats are doing. This is unlike the over reactive reporting against Republicans on MSNBC. If you want the truth or something close to the truth, you need to form your opinion watching these three mainstream media channels. The truth is in the middle. That's my experience anyway!

Better yet would be going "to the horse's mouth" as they used to say. Go to the government's websites (house.gov or senate.gov) and read the text of the bill or law yourself! Another good place for this would be watching C-Span when they are carrying the U. S. House of Representatives and U. S. Senate live. C-Span also often replays the daily recorded live program in the evening as well as sometimes the middle of the night. They have a daily archive too! There is even a daily call-in program with dedicated call-in numbers. For instance, a Republican line, a Democrat line, and an Independent line.

This is just a bit of the news I watch analyzed here. However, I also watch PBS often as well as Canadian, British, and Japanese News Broadcasts. Now add the news I read on Yahoo, The LA Times, The Huffington Post, Local TV Stations, and The New York Times to name a few. You will see that I'm a news junkie and well informed. Oh yeah, I also listen to talk radio!

"Should I list some?", I laughingly ask. Of course, I didn't mention social media. Laughs again!

Unfortunately, many of you don't have this kind of time so I'm working on solutions! I often have news on in the background while doing dishes, dusting, and otherwise cleaning house. This doesn't work well with young children nor do I recommend it. No need to terrify or depress our kids. Though as teens 14 and older, the approximate high school Freshman's age up, I do recommend it for them. Afterall, they will be adults soon with the ability, even the right and duty to vote. As parents of teens, we have a responsibility to teach them to be informed voters. We also have a responsibility to teach the respectful exchange of ideas and opinions!

Another solution idea is in my book, <u>Rain's Realm: The Future In Bloom</u>. That would be the TV debate idea as well as the proposed 28th Amendment to "The Constitution of the United States of America". These ideas are much harder to implement. The 28th Amendment requires Congress to do their job first and "We the People" to then do ours and ratify it. Of course, "We the People" can pressure Congress to get it done and on the ballots for voting in 2018! On the down side, the TV debate idea takes support, funding, and a time slot of a broadcaster. Plus there would be other supports of production. On the plus side, it would create a few jobs?!

Minus changing how government works now, I have one more solution to the be informed and have time to do so problem. It's the "Women Working Wonders Wednesdays" idea as explained in this book. The Women Working Wonders Wednesdays idea is created for groups of up to thirty women who are ages 14 years and up. Each time a group reaches more than thirty women, they branch off to a new group. The leader of the new group having come from the branching off group.

When I originally wrote this back in 2012, I had twelve categories. I have since decided to add categories. It was July 4, 2017 when I made this decision. As always, I was watching news and celebrations of America's 241st Birthday. We Americans had the previous year been through the worst Presidential election of my life time! I had heard stereotypes and accusations of who Americans are that I hadn't heard since the 70's. Some I had never heard and were worse than previously heard accusations. All of the accusations were used to create division! The accusations divided by age, race, sex, religion, class, political party, and any other division they could think of. To some extent, WE THE PEOPLE ALLOWED this! Had many people not reacted to or believed the accusations then the news media would have changed tactics. Had "We the People" been more educated and/or connected to each other at least locally, the media would not have been able to cause such division. That is why I decided to add two categories and expand on one from the time I originally wrote this idea to its publishing in 2018.

Each group will have the following categories:

1. Their leader.

2. President watcher-whitehouse.gov

3. U.S. House of Representatives watcher-house.gov

4. U.S. Senate watcher-senate.gov

5. Governor watcher

6. State House of
   Representatives watcher

7. State Senate watcher

8. School Board watcher

9. Township watcher

10. City-Mayor watcher

11. Coupon Clipper

12. Misc News Reporter
    expanded to a person each
    for:

    a. CNN

    b. MSNBC

    c. Fox News

13. UN watcher- un.org

14. Foreign News watcher and
    possibly based on specific
    countries.

2 HOW IT WORKS

The Leader should be an older woman and know the U.S. Constitution as well as understand why it was written the way it was. She obviously runs each meeting on Wednesdays. Suggested time from 7:00pm to 9:00pm, but can choose other hours if they work better for her and the other women in her group. She "calls the meeting to order". She asks for each report starting with the report of the President. She decides if more needs to be done such as phone calls, e-mails, news alerts, social media posts, etc. She doesn't decide on her own, however. She decides with the group. Because if action is taken, the whole group takes the action. They decide to call the President so all thirty women call the President for example. (Or how many women are currently in the group.) She goes down the list in the same way.

Women in positions 2. through 10. and 13. do the following: Each woman spends one hour per week "watching" their assigned or volunteered for person or branch of government. They research through the government websites what is happening, bills presented, read the bills, take notes, and make comments to present to the group. Comments should be both good and bad so the group can make an informed decision. Leaders may decided to research more on their own before asking the group what they'd like to do. The group can also ask the Leader to do more research to help them understand and decide.

Women in position 11. The Coupon Clipper do the following: The Coupon Clipper collects unwanted coupons from members. Members could put them in a small box, bucket, or container of some sort as they come in. Then the Coupon Clipper takes them home, cuts them out, and organizes them. She then brings them back so after the meeting, members can take what they'll use on their way out.

Some suggestions to organize them would be using an expanding file folder, a bucket of clasp envelopes, or a larger bucket with smaller plastic containers. Organize them within those folders, envelopes, or containers by month, name brand, type, or a combination of the above. By type, I mean like by cereal, baby, cleaners, and so forth. Maybe she's a better organizer than me and figures out something better. If so, sharing her skills with other groups would be wonderful!

The Coupon Clipper MAY also watch for other deals in the community and make a report during the meeting. An example of this would be the Michigan Park Pass that can be purchased on the Plate Renewal. It has discounts available at retailers and businesses through-out Michigan. Show your car's registration as proof-of-purchase to get the deal or discount. To find current offerings as of this search in August 2017, go to:
<u>www.michigan.gov/passportperks</u>

Women in positions 12. and 14. do the following: Miscellaneous and Foreign News Reporters was pretty self-explanatory when I first wrote this. Actually, I added the Foreign News Reporter since writing this in 2012 as explained in the Introduction. Therefore, I'm editing and adding more here as I go along. As I put in the list above, there would be more reporters than I originally wrote about. There would definitely be a CNN reporter, an MSNBC reporter, and a FOX News reporter as well as the original Miscellaneous reporter and the Foreign reporter. Of course, these reporters collect news they think would be of interest to members and report it each week. They collect news from multiple sources- tv, radio, internet, newspapers, word-of-mouth, etc. If the news is word-of-mouth, they need to guard against gossip! Love, Always Love; and "Do unto others as you'd have done unto you":) This is great advice for all members;)

Here is some more guidance for the Foreign Reporter. Have a main Foreign Reporter who does the above news collecting for countries outside of the United States or the main country if this goes into other countries. If she sees a country that needs more attention then she can ask for a specific country reporter. An example at this time would be North Korea because of all the missiles they are sending up. The group might suggest sending e-mails and making calls to their Senators to express concern and be sure that their Senators are concerned as well. The Senate watchers might do this rather than the whole group and share the Senators' responses at the next meeting. Then after the response decide whether or not to take further action.

The Leader can make more Watchers/ Teachers, but these are the minimum to help keep our government working for We the People, because the government will KNOW MANY are watching and KNOW what they're doing. Depending on the members make-up, beliefs, and/or interests, some other Watchers/

Teachers might be some of the following:

Financial- advice, how to budget, record keeping, taxes and laws that apply to most of the group's members, and any other financial help for the group.

Prayer- collect prayer requests and pray for members.

Church Liaison- take notes during the meeting and prepare a short notice for members to give to Religious Leaders for reading to Congregations or copying and inserting with the Churches' Bulletin.

Charity Liaison- maintains a list of local charities and rotates donations to them. Again, the Leader knows her group best and can make suggestions. Members can of course make suggestions too!

The Leader summarizes the meeting while members take notes or check their notes on actions to be taken. Then she passes around a Happy Hat. Members may make financial donations, prayer requests, and/or leave messages of happiness, praise, or encouragement. A portion of financial donations will go to refreshments and a portion to local charities on a rotating basis. Also, near the beginning of the first Women Working Wonders Wednesdays, she will secure pocket copies of the Constitution for current members and as more members are added. Leaders that are in branch-off groups would then have their copies and be responsible for securing copies for their new members. Depending again on the members' interests, beliefs, make-up, etc.; she may offer a prayer, message of her own, or pick a message from the Happy Hat before saying she'll see them next week. After the Leader says she'll see them next week, members may remain briefly (up to 30 minutes?) for refreshments, chat, and coupon gathering.

3 AFTER THE MEETING

The Leader keeps 20% per week of any financial donations and buys the next week's refreshments. She also makes a 10% donation as explained earlier to the rotating charities unless she appointed someone. She spends at least one hour per week preparing for the next meeting, doing research which includes checking our Government's and Women Working Wonders Wednesdays Group's actions are inline with the Constitution, enjoying messages from the "Happy Hat" and answering prayer requests by praying. She also prepares the next week's opening or "Call to Order" :) If she finds group actions are not inline with the Constitution, she informs the Women Working Wonders Wednesdays Group after opening greetings at the next meeting. She then asks if the members want to take a different action. Of course, since the Leader knows the

Constitution, and it's part of the discussion on taking action or not; this is not likely to happen. If the Government is not inline with the Constitution, she brings it to the Group's attention and asks for action(s) to be taken. She also takes any decided action(s).

Leaders may wish to ask members for e-mail and phone numbers for emergency cancellation mainly and give hers to the members for the same. Keep Women Working Wonders Wednesdays Group notes off the pc and in written notebooks or best of all in member's heads! Maybe I'm being paranoid? At least, be safe! There are too many hackers and stalkers at this time and possibly in the future as well. It's also easier to review notes in a notebook.

A good place to purchase the Constitution is:

https://nccs.net/product/bulk-pocket-constitutions

As of August 16, 2017, you can get 100 copies for $40 and FREE shipping.

OR

If you want copies that look more like the little Bibles kids are given:

<u>https://store.cato.org/book/cato-pocket-</u>

<u>constitution-0</u>

That takes you directly to The Pocket Constitution. If it doesn't because of changes to the site since this search in 2017, search "The Pocket Constitution". They are available in Spanish and Arabic too! Bulk pricing is also available. The above link takes you to the 10 copies for $10 as of August 16, 2017.

Thank-you for your purchase and best wishes to you and your Women Working Wonders Wednesdays Group!! :) :) May we all be more knowledgeable of our Governments from the local, to the state, to the federal, and to the world and make the world more Wonderful!! :) :)

4 A WORD ABOUT THE CONSTITUTION

While you wait for your copies of the Constitution to arrive for your group, here's a little bit to get you started. Many of you know the 1st Amendment. Some of you know the 1st Amendment means EVERYONE has freedom of speech, freedom of religion, and freedom of the press as well as the freedom to PEACEFULLY assemble and to tell our government what we don't like or how we want things changed. However, do you know WHY these things are in the Constitution and HOW the writers of the Constitution meant for them to work?

As we were taught in history, the King and Church of England were in control of everything. The King made the laws. The King was head of the Church of England so even though he often took advice from other church clerics, he still made the laws. Also, of course, it was widely believed that the King and his family were of "special blood" so this made them better than other people. Being born into royalty gave you the right to rule over others with the Church of England when your turn came. Well, many people being ruled by the King and Church disagreed!

Some of the people being ruled started talking about their disagreements with the King and the Church of England. As they realized they were not alone in their disagreement they started meeting together. These meetings grew and formed another church. The Protestant Church began. This is a simplified explanation of religious change as many other factors were part of the creation of the Church of England, but we don't need to know all of that for our purposes here. Also, as more and more of the people talked among themselves, the King and Church of England heard about it. They started quietly trying to stop the disagreements. Unfortunately, this lead to widespread religious persecution.

To get away from this religious persecution, many Protestants became what we know of today to be refugees! Much of history calls them Pilgrims. They originally went to other countries outside of the King's rule. Often they were treated as outsiders and expected to live and believe as the people of their new countries lived and believed. (Hmm...kind of like refugees today too huh?) Some did decide they liked their new country and could accept its ways of life. Others could not. They also didn't want their children to accept it. It was at that time they heard about "ships going to a new land".

They decided to go to the new land. Although everyone on the boats were going to the same new land, the reasons for going were very different. Some, like the persecuted refugee Pilgrims, were going to preserve their beliefs and ways of life. Others were on the ships seeking to get rich or merely for adventure. Once arriving in the new land, now known as the United States of America, many like-minded people stayed together and settled together.

I'm not going the rest of the way through history because I've reminded you already of the religious war, persecuted beliefs, sharing of ideas (assembly), being created equal, and desire for freedom and self directed lives. It was knowledge of this history, honoring this history, and a strong desire to make a world free of war that our Constitution of the United States of America was based upon. It was a desire for peace and for freedom from government and church control of "We the People".

The writers of the Constitution had many debates while writing it. They decided man was basically good, but needed LIMITED government to protect people from the unlawful, misguided, or new people. They wrote the Constitution so varying beliefs could be shared PEACEFULLY and LEGALLY, but also so it would be the "like-minded", "way of life" document we could all agree to live with for the "Pursuit of life, liberty, and happiness". This "Spirit of the Constitution" is just as true and important today as it was when it was written! Maybe even more so?!

ABOUT THE AUTHOR

RainBlue owns Rain's Realm LLC which has not had its "brick and mortar" home yet. She shares her real name with an already published author, photographer, and social activist! This and the fact that she has been online chatting and posting since 1993, mostly under the nick RainBlue is the reason she published under this pen name. Since using the nick, she has learned that Rain stands for "Life giver or teacher" and Blue for "Healer" among Native American and spiritual cultures. She feels the nick is perfect for her!

She is also a very proud Mother and Grandmother! She has numerous interests and hobbies as well as a deep desire to make the world a better place to live for many generations; even all time. She lives in the extremely beautiful Upper Peninsula of Michigan in the United States of America.

www.ingramcontent.com/pod-product-compliance
Lightning Source LLC
Chambersburg PA
CBHW050806240726
48654CB00008B/656